BULLETPOINTS

BRITISH HISTORY

John Farndon
Consultant: Richard Tames

First published in 2003 by Miles Kelly Publishing Ltd
Bardfield Centre, Great Bardfield
Essex, CM7 4SL

2 4 6 8 10 9 7 5 3

Editor: Ruthie Boardman

Design: Debbie Meekcoms

Picture Research: Liberty Newton

Assistant: Carol Danenbergs

Production: Estela Godoy

British Library Cataloguing-in-Publication Data
A catalogue record for this book is available from the British Library

ISBN 1-84236-260-7

Printed in China

www.mileskelly.net
info@mileskelly.net

The publishers would like to thank the following artists who have contributed to this book:
Peter Dennis, Nicholas Forder, Terry Gabbey, Studio Galante, Sally Holmes, Richard Hook
Angus McBride, Terry Riley, Martin Sanders, Guy Smith, Nick Spender, Rudi Vizi, Mike White
All other pictures are from: MKP archives; Corel; DigitalSTOCK; digitalvision; PhotoDisc

Contents

The first Britons

- **Britain** has been inhabited by human-like creatures for over 500,000 years. The oldest known settlement, at Star Carr in Yorkshire, dates back 10,000 years.

- **About 6–7000** years ago, Neolithic farmers arrived from Europe. They began to clear the island's thick woods to grow crops and build houses in stone.

- **The early farmers** created round monuments of stones and wooden posts called *henges*. The most famous is Stonehenge in Wiltshire.

- **c.2300BC,** new people from the Rhine arrived. They are called Beakerfolk, after their beaker-shaped pottery cups. They were Britain's first metal-workers.

- **Legend** has it that the name Britain came from Brutus, one of the sons of Aeneas, who fled from Troy.

- **c.700BC,** Celts arrived, often living in hillforts.

- **Iron axes** and ploughs enabled huge areas to be cleared and farmed, and the population rose.

- **When Julius Caesar** invaded, in 55 and 54BC, the Celtic people of England, called Britons, were divided into scores of tribes, such as the Catuvellauni and Atrebates.

- **Resistance** from tribal leaders such as Caratacus meant it took the Romans over a century to conquer the Britons.

- **The last** revolt was that of Queen Boudicca, in AD60.

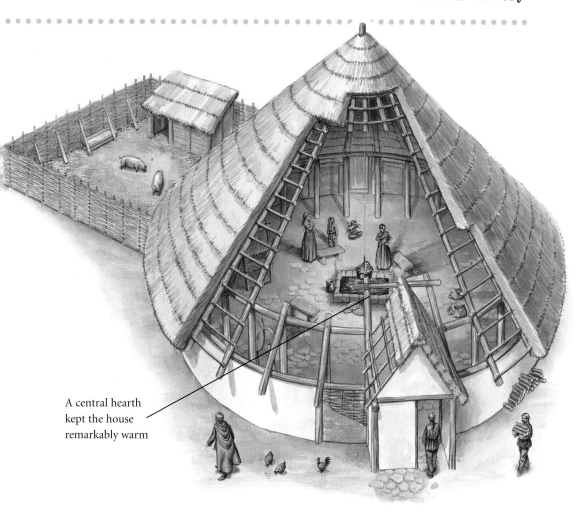

A central hearth
kept the house
remarkably warm

▲ *People of Bronze Age Britain lived in round houses like this,
with thick stone walls and a steeply-pitched, thatched roof.*

Early English kings

- **Egbert, king of Wessex** from AD802 to 839, became in effect the first king of England when he conquered Mercia at Ellandun in 829. But his rule lasted just a year before the Mercian king, Wiglaf, claimed Mercia back.

- **For 100 years,** much of England was lost to the Danes, but Alfred the Great's son Edward and his daughter Aethelflaed gradually drove the Danes out by 918.

- **England's kingship** really began with Athelstan, crowned 'King of all Britain' at Kingston on September 4, 925.

- **'Ethelred the Unready'** was king of England 978–1013 and 1014–1016. *Rede* was old English for advice, and his name meant he was always badly advised.

- **Ethelred created** so much distrust among his subjects that the Danes easily reconquered England in 980.

- **In 1013**, Dane Sweyn Forkbeard became king of England.

- **When** Sweyn died, Ethelred made a comeback until Sweyn's son, Canute, drove him out. Canute became king of England in 1016 by marrying Ethelred's widow, Emma.

▲ *King Canute*

- **Canute ruled well.** A story tells how he rebuked flatterers by showing how even he could not stop the tide coming in.

- **After Canute,** in 1035, came Harold I (1035–40, followed by Harthacanute (1040–42). Ethelred's son, Edward the Confessor, then became king – but the Danes did not want a Saxon king.

- **The Danes** called on their Norwegian allies, led first by Magnus then Harold Hardraada, to win back the throne.

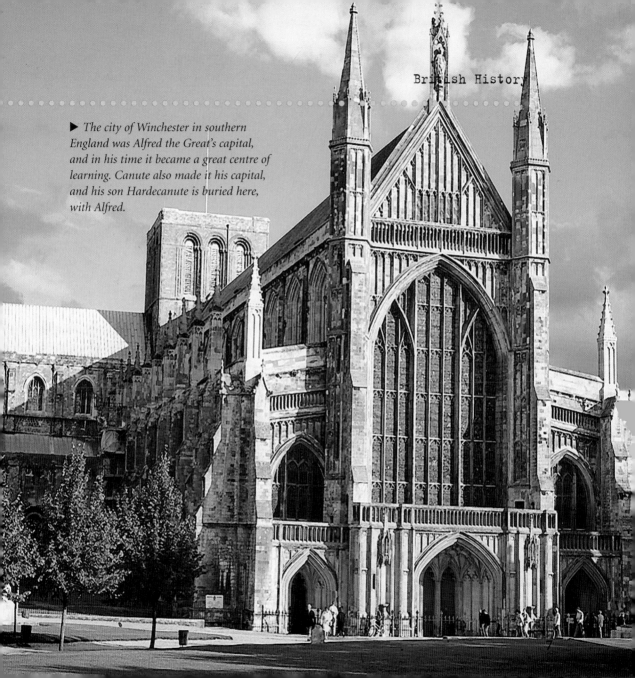

▶ *The city of Winchester in southern England was Alfred the Great's capital, and in his time it became a great centre of learning. Canute also made it his capital, and his son Hardecanute is buried here, with Alfred.*

The Norman invasion

- **On 5 January 1066,** the English king Edward the Confessor died. As he died, he named as his successor Harold Godwinson – the powerful earl of the kingdom of Wessex.

▲ *William's troops rapidly seized control of England. This was the last time the country was conquered by a foreign power.*

- **Harold's claim** to the English throne was challenged by William, the duke of Normandy in France, who claimed that Edward had already promised him the throne.

- **Harold's claim** was also challenged by Harold Hardraade (the Ruthless), the king of Norway.

- **In autumn 1066,** Hardraade invaded northern England with Harold Godwinson's brother Tostig. His army was routed by Harold's at Stamford Bridge on 25 September.

- **On 27 Sept,** William's Norman army of 7000 crossed from France and landed at Pevensey in S. England.

- **Harold marched** his army south to meet the Normans, walking over 300 km to London in just five days.

▲ *The Normans commemorated their victory at the Battle of Hastings with a famous tapestry, made in England, now in Bayeux in France.*

- **Harold's tired army** met the Normans at Hastings in Sussex on the 14th of October, and took a stand by the Hoar Apple Tree on Caldbec Hill.

- **Harold's army** was mauled by William's archers, but axe-wielding English house–carles (infantry) put the Norman cavalry to flight. Harold was then killed – perhaps by an arrow. The English fought on for a while before fleeing.

- **After the battle** William moved on London, where he was crowned king in Westminster Abbey on 25 December.

- **Within a few years**, the Normans had conquered England.

The Magna Carta

- **John I** was king of England from 1199–1216. He was one of the most unpopular kings in history.

- **John was nicknamed** 'Lackland' by his father Henry II because, unlike his older brothers Richard and Geoffrey, he did not inherit land to provide him with an income.

- **John was hated** for his cruelty, for the demands he put on his barons for tax and military service and for trying to seize the crown while his popular brother King Richard the Lionheart was Crusading.

- **On 15 June 1215,** rebellious barons compelled John to meet them at Runnymede on the Thames and agree to their demands by sealing the Magna Carta ('Great Charter').

- **Ordinary people** gained little at the time from the Magna Carta but it is now seen as the world's first bill of rights and the start of fair government in England.

- **The Magna Carta** showed that even the king had to obey the law.

- **Magna Carta** contained 63 clauses, most relating to feudal customs.

- **Clause 39** gave every free man the right to a fair trial. Clause 40 gave everyone the right to instant justice.

- **Some parts of** the Magna Carta dealt with weights and measures, foreign merchants and catching fish.

- **John got the pope** to annul the document three days later, but it was reissued in 1225, after John's death.

▼ *The barons compelled King John to put his seal (wax stamp) on the Magna Carta at Runnymede in 1215.*

Bannockburn

- **In 1286, King Alexander III** of Scotland died. His grandaughter – Margaret, 'Maid of Norway' – died four years later. Their deaths left no obvious successor to the Scottish throne.

- **The Scottish lords** agreed to the suggestion of English king Edward I that he should decide between the 13 rival claimants, including John de Balliol and Robert Bruce.

- **Edward I** marched into Scotland, imprisoned the leading claimant John deBalliol and declared himself king. Some of Balliol's rivals, such as Robert, supported Edward.

- **The Scottish lords** did not react, but a small landowner called William Wallace began a heroic fight. With a band of just 30 men, he attacked Lanark, took the garrison and killed the English sheriff. Commoners flocked to his aid.

- **On 4 May 1297,** Wallace's small rebel army scored a stunning victory over the English at Stirling. He drove the English from Scotland and marched on into England. But the Scottish lords still gave him no support.

  - **Wallace** was captured by the English in 1305. He was hanged, drawn (disembowelled) and quartered (cut in four pieces). His head was stuck on a pole on London Bridge.

  - **Wallace's** heroism inspired Robert Bruce to lead a rebellion that finally included the Scottish lords.

◀ The story goes that, while in hiding, Robert Bruce was inspired to go on fighting after seeing a spider struggle up its thread again and again – and eventually succeed.

- **Letting his enemies** think he was dead, Robert launched a campaign from Ireland in 1306. Within two years he had cleared the English from Scotland again.

- **Robert scored** a last decisive victory over the English under Edward II at Bannockburn on 23–24 June 1314. With this victory, the Scots regained their independence.

▼ *Scottish hero Robert Bruce freed the Scots from English control at the Battle of Bannockburn, in 1314.*

. . . **FASCINATING FACT** . . .
At Bannockburn, just 5000 Scots may have routed an English army of 23,000.

The Hundred Years' War

- **The Hundred Years' War** was a long war between France and England, lasting from 1337–1453.

- **The war** was caused by disputes over Guyenne (English land in southwest France), English claims to the French throne, French support for the Scots and French efforts to block the English wool trade in Belgium.

- **1337:** French king Philip VI tried to take over Guyenne. English king Edward III, whose mother was sister to three French kings, retaliated by claiming the French throne.

  - **1340:** Edward won a great naval battle off Sluis, Belgium.

    - **1346:** Edward III's archers – outnumbered 3 to 1 – routed the greatest French knights at Crécy with their great 2-m-long yew bows, and so hastened the end of knighthood.

      - **1347:** Edward III took the French port of Calais.

      - **1356:** Edward III's son, the Black Prince, won a great victory over the French at Poitiers.

    - **1415:** the last great English victory was Henry V's at Agincourt; 6000 English beat a French army of 30,000.

    - **The English** won most battles, but the French won the war because they had three times the resources.

◄ *The greatest knight of the war was Edward the Black Prince (1330–76), hero of the Battles of Crécy, Poitiers and Navarette.*

▲ *In the Battle of Agincourt (1415),*
the French failed to learn lessons
from previous defeats and
Henry V won a glorious victory.

· · · **FASCINATING FACT** · · ·
The tide turned for the French in 1429, when
Joan of Arc led them to victory at Orléans.

The Wars of the Roses

- **The Wars of the Roses** were a series of civil wars fought in England in the 1400s as two branches of the Plantagenet family fought for the English throne.

- **On one side** was the house of York, with a white rose as its emblem. On the other was the house of Lancaster, with a red rose as its emblem.

- **The wars began** when Lancastrian king Henry VI became insane in 1453. With the country in chaos, Warwick the 'kingmaker' set up Richard, duke of York as Protector in Henry's place.

- **In 1455, Henry VI** seemed to recover and war broke out between Lancastrians and Yorkists.

  - **Richard** was killed at the Battle of Wakefield in 1460, but Henry VI became insane again.

    - **A crushing Yorkist victory** at Towton, near York, in 1461, put Richard's son on the throne as Edward IV.

    - **Edward IV** made enemies of his brothers Clarence and Warwick, who invaded England from France in 1470 with Henry VI's queen Margaret of Anjou and drove Edward out.

▲ *The white – and red – roses were emblems of the rival houses of York and Lancaster. When Henry VII wed Elizabeth of York, he combined the two to make the Tudor rose.*

- **Henry VI** was brought back for seven months before Edward's Yorkists defeated the Lancastrians at Barnet and Tewkesbury. Henry VI was murdered.

- **When Edward IV** died in 1483, his son Edward V was still a boy. When young, Edward and his brother vanished – probably murdered in the Tower of London – and their uncle Richard III seized the throne.

- **Richard III** made enemies among the Yorkists, who sided with Lancastrian Henry Tudor. Richard III was killed at Bosworth Field on 22 August 1485. Henry Tudor became Henry VII and married Elizabeth of York to end the wars.

▲ *Richard was a harsh man, but not the evil monster portrayed in Shakespeare's play,* Richard III.

Henry VIII

- **Henry VIII** (1491–1547) was the Tudor king of England who separated the Church in England from Rome, and who married six wives, beheading two of them.

- **Henry's wives:** Catherine of Aragon (1509–33, divorced); Anne Boleyn (1533–36, beheaded); Jane Seymour (1536–38, died); Anne of Cleves (1540, annulled); Catherine Howard (1540–42, beheaded); and Catherine Parr (1543–47).

- **When Henry VIII** became king at 18, in 1509, he was handsome and athletic, spoke several languages, played the lute well and was keen on new 'humanist' ideas. As he grew old, he became grossly fat, riddled with sickness and inclined to terrible outbreaks of anger.

- **Henry was served** by clever ministers like Wolsey and Cromwell. Many were executed when things went wrong.

◄ *We have an astonishingly clear picture of what Henry and his court looked like from the brilliant portraits of Hans Holbein. This picture is based on Holbein's striking painting of Henry from 1537.*

▶ *Catherine Parr – the only one of Henry VIII's six wives to survive him.*

- **Catherine of Aragon** bore Henry a daughter, Mary, but not the needed son. The pope refused a divorce, so Henry broke with Rome to become head of the English Church.

- **Split from Rome,** the Church of England moved towards Protestantism and the monasteries were destroyed.

- **Anne Boleyn** gave Henry a daughter, Elizabeth, but not the son he wanted, and her strong views made her enemies. She was beheaded on a charge of treason.

- **Jane Seymour** gave Henry a son, Edward, but died in childbirth in 1538.

- **Henry** found Anne of Cleves so ugly, he cancelled the marriage after five months.

- **Young Catherine Howard** was beheaded when she was found to have a lover. Only Henry's last wife, twice-widowed Catherine Parr, survived him when he died in 1547.

Elizabeth I

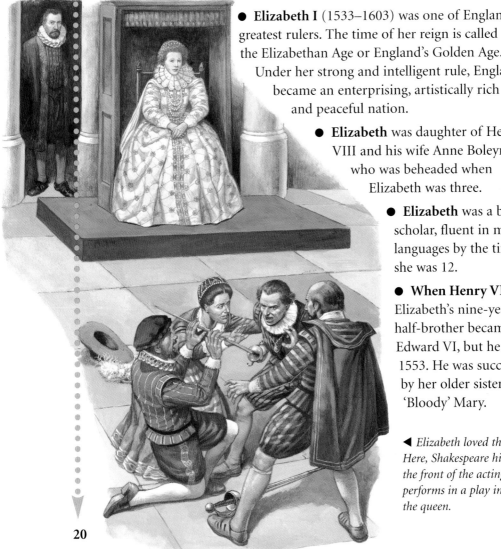

- **Elizabeth I** (1533–1603) was one of England's greatest rulers. The time of her reign is called the Elizabethan Age or England's Golden Age. Under her strong and intelligent rule, England became an enterprising, artistically rich and peaceful nation.

- **Elizabeth** was daughter of Henry VIII and his wife Anne Boleyn, who was beheaded when Elizabeth was three.

- **Elizabeth** was a brilliant scholar, fluent in many languages by the time she was 12.

- **When Henry VIII died,** Elizabeth's nine-year-old half-brother became King Edward VI, but he died in 1553. He was succeeded by her older sister 'Bloody' Mary.

◀ *Elizabeth loved the theatre. Here, Shakespeare himself (at the front of the acting group) performs in a play in front of the queen.*

▶ *William Shakespeare was one of several important English writers whose work flourished during Elizabeth I's reign.*

- **Mary was** staunchly Catholic. For a while Elizabeth was locked up, suspected of involvement in a Protestant plot.

- **Elizabeth became queen** in 1558, when Mary died.

- **At once** Elizabeth strengthened the Protestant Church of England by the Act of Supremacy in 1559.

- **Elizabeth was expected** to marry, and she encouraged foreign suitors when it helped diplomacy. But she remained single, earning her the nickname 'The Virgin Queen'.

- **Elizabeth** sent troops to help Protestants in Holland against their Spanish rulers, and secretly urged Francis Drake to raid Spanish treasure ships. In 1588 Spain sent an Armada to invade England. Elizabeth proved an inspiring leader and the Armada was repulsed.

- **Elizabeth's reign** is famed for the poetry and plays of men like Spenser, Marlowe and Shakespeare.

Mary Queen of Scots

- **Mary Queen of Scots** (1542–87) was the Catholic queen of Scotland held captive in England by Elizabeth I for 19 years, then beheaded.

- **Mary became queen** when she was a baby but was brought up at the French court, where she enjoyed hunting and learned six languages.

- **Mary married** the French king Henry II's son Francis at 15 and was briefly queen of France, but Francis died in 1560.

- **In 1561,** Mary returned to Scotland to rule there. By this time, Scotland had become Protestant, while Mary was a Catholic.

- **In 1565,** Mary fell in love with her cousin Henry Stuart, Earl of Darnley. She married him and they had a child, but Darnley was only interested in power.

- **Led by Darnley,** Protestant nobles stabbed Mary's Catholic secretary David Rizzio to death before her.

- **The Earl of Bothwell** was in love with Mary and murdered Darnley. They married three months later. The Scots were so outraged by the marriage that Mary had to flee to England.

◀ *Mary with her cousin and second husband, the highly ambitious Earl of Darnley – an ill-starred marriage that ended in deception and double murder.*

- **Mary was next in line** to the English throne after Elizabeth. Many Catholics felt she was first in line, since they did not recognize Henry VIII's marriage to Anne Boleyn.

- **Mary posed a danger** to Elizabeth, so she was kept in captivity in English houses, where she became the focus for plots against Elizabeth.

- **Elizabeth's spy-master** Walsingham trapped Mary into going along with a plot by Babington. Mary was found guilty of treason and beheaded at Fotheringay in 1587.

▶ *Mary about to meet her death at the executioner's block. Her presence in England had made her a dangerous focus for Catholic plots against Elizabeth I.*

Roundheads and Cavaliers

- **The English Civil War** (1642–49) was the struggle between 'Cavalier' supporters of King Charles I and 'Roundheads', who supported Parliament.

- **A key issue** was how much power the king should have. Charles wanted to be free to set taxes and his own brand of religion. Parliament demanded a say.

- **On the royalist side** were those, who wanted the English Church more Catholic; on the other were Puritans.

- **Puritans** were extreme Protestants. They believed that churches (and people) should be stripped of the wasteful luxury they saw in the Catholic Church and the aristocrats at the court of Charles's French, Catholic wife.

- **'Cavalier'** is from the French *chevalier* (horseman). It was meant as a term of abuse. Many Cavaliers were rich landowners.

- **Puritans** thought long hair indulgent, and the Roundheads got their name from their short-cropped hair. Many Roundheads were rich merchants and townspeople.

▶ *A Cavalier soldier. The term Cavalier was coined because many of Charles's supporters were seen as frivolous courtiers who loved fighting for its own sake.*

- **Many revolutionary groups** emerged among poorer people, such as the 'Diggers' and 'Levellers'.

- **The war** turned against the royalists when the parliamentarians formed the disciplined New Model Army.

- **Charles I** was beheaded in 1649.

- **Oliver Cromwell** (1599–1658) became Roundhead leader and signed Charles I's death warrant. In 1653, he made himself Lord Protector – England's dictator.

▶ *Many Cavaliers had long hair and wore colourful and elaborate clothes after the style of the French court. Some, like Lovelace, were poets.*

The Restoration

- **For 11 years** after the execution of Charles I in 1649, England was without a king. It was ruled instead by the Commonwealth, run by the Puritans.

- **At first,** the Commonwealth consisted of Parliament and its Council of State, but its failure to make progress spurred general Oliver Cromwell to make himself Lord Protector and rule through army officers.

- **Cromwell's Protectorate** proved unpopular. When he died in 1658, the army removed his son Richard Cromwell as successor and called for Charles I's exiled son Charles II to be recalled as king.

- **The Restoration** of Charles II as king was in May 1660.

- **Charles II** proved on the whole a skilful ruler, tactfully easing tensions between rival religious groups.

- **Charles II** was known as the Merry Monarch, because his love of partying, theatre, horse-racing and women was such a relief after years of grim Puritan rule.

▶ *The sedan chair was a popular way for the rich to get about in the years after the Restoration.*

- **Charles II** had many mistresses. The most famous was Nell Gwyn, an orange-seller who worked in the theatre.

- **The Restoration** saw the Puritan ban on Christmas and the theatre lifted. Plays like Congreve's *Way of the World* made Restoration theatre lively and outrageous.

- **Charles II** took a keen interest in science, encouraging great scientists like Isaac Newton, Edmund Halley and Robert Hooke to form the Royal Society.

▲ *Exiled after his father's death, Charles first attempted to bring back the monarchy in 1651 but was defeated. After nine more years in exile, he was finally invited to return as king.*

...FASCINATING FACT...
When London burned down, in 1666, Charles II personally organized the fire-fighting.

The Glorious Revolution

- **The Glorious Revolution** of 1688 was when the English Parliament replaced James II with William III and Mary, as king and queen.

- **James II** became king when his brother Charles II died in 1685.

- **James II** upset people by giving Catholics key jobs in the army, the Church and the universities.

- **James II** jailed any bishops who refused to support his Declaration of Indulgence in favour of Catholics.

- **In 1688,** James II and his Catholic wife Mary had a son. It seemed England was set to become Catholic.

- **Leading Protestants** decided to invite the Dutch prince William of Orange to help. William was married to James II's Protestant daughter Mary.

◄ *Mary sided with her Protestant husband, William, against her Catholic father James II.*

- **William landed** with his army at Brixham in Devon on 5 November 1688. James's army refused to obey its Catholic generals and so he was forced to flee to France.

- **Parliament** decided James's escape meant he had abdicated, and offered the throne to William and Mary.

- **James** tried a comeback, landing in Ireland with French troops. Defeat came at the Battle of the Boyne (July 1689).

▶ *William III, or William of Orange (1650-1702), suffered much political opposition and countless assassination plots in the latter years of his reign.*

William III

. . . **FASCINATING FACT** . . .
Ulster Protestants are called Orangemen because they once helped William of Orange at the Boyne.

The Industrial Revolution

- **The Industrial Revolution** refers to the dramatic growth in factories that began in the 1700s.

- **Before the Industrial Revolution**, most ordinary people were farmers living in small villages. Afterwards, most were factory hands and foremen living in huge cities.

- **The Revolution** began in Britain in the late 1700s; in France, the USA and Germany in the early 1800s.

- **The Farming Revolution** created a pool of cheap labour, while the growth of European colonies created vast markets for things like clothing.

- **The Revolution** began with the invention of machines for making cloth, like the spinning jenny.

- **The turning point** was the change from hand-turned machines like the jenny to machines driven by big water wheels – like Arkwright's 'water powered spinning frame' of 1766.

- **In 1771,** Arkwright installed water frames at Crompton Mill, Derby and created the world's first big factory.

◀ *In 1764, Lancashire weaver James Hargreaves created the 'spinning jenny' to help cottage weavers spin wool or cotton fibres into yarn (thread) on lots of spindles, turned by a single handle.*

- **In the 1780s**, James Watt developed a steam engine to drive machines – and steam engines quickly replaced water as the main source of power in factories.

- **In 1713,** Abraham Darby found how to use coke, rather than wood charcoal, to make huge amounts of iron.

- **In 1784,** Henry Cort found how to remove impurities from cast iron to make wrought iron – and iron became the key material of the Industrial Revolution.

▶ *Arkwright's water frame, powered by a water wheel, used four pairs of rotating rollers to stretch fibres before they were spun.*

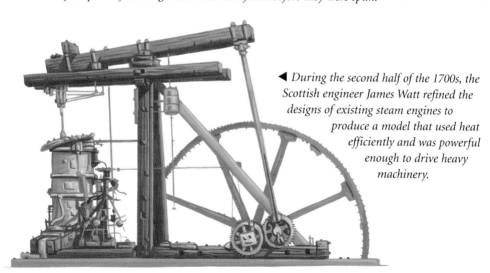

◀ *During the second half of the 1700s, the Scottish engineer James Watt refined the designs of existing steam engines to produce a model that used heat efficiently and was powerful enough to drive heavy machinery.*

31

The British Empire

- **At its height,** in 1920, the British Empire covered a quarter of the world and ruled a quarter of the world's population.

- **The British** ruled more peoples than any other nation.

- **The British Empire** began to build up in the 1600s, as British merchants started to extend their trading links throughout the world. The British won out over Dutch, Portuguese, French and Belgian rivals through the success of their navy and also their reasonably efficient colonial government.

- **The 13 American colonies** broke away in 1776, but Canada and many West Indian islands remained British.

- **Britain** gained control of India through the East India Company, between 1757 and 1858. In 1877, Queen Victoria was proclaimed Empress of India – the first time the word empire had been used in relation to the British possessions.

- **Many of the British possessions** had similar climates to Britain's – parts of Canada, South Africa, Australia and New Zealand – and British settlers moved to these places in huge numbers in the 1900s, pushing out the native inhabitants. These colonies were given more and more freedom to govern themselves and came to be called 'dominions'.

- **The Empire** reached its peak after World War 1, when German and Turkish possessions were added.

- **After World War 2,** more countries demanded independence. India and Pakistan became independent in 1947, Ceylon in 1948. By 1980, most African, West Indian and Pacific Island colonies were independent.

◀ *The British Empire was controlled by the British navy and army. The army worked in every continent, from India to Egypt, and Australia to Canada.*

● **Most colonies** remained within the Commonwealth after independence. There are 54 Commonwealth nations, linked essentially by agreed principles, but they all accept the British queen as head of the Commonwealth.

▲ *This map shows the British Empire in the 1930s, when it was beginning to shrink. Egypt was given some independence in 1922, when Sultan Ahmed became King Fuad I. Iraq gained a similar independence when amir Ahd Allah Faisal became King Faisal I.*

. . . FASCINATING FACT . . .
In 1920, 600 million people around the
world were ruled from London.

Victorian England

- **In 1837,** 18-year-old Victoria became the queen of England and reigned for 63 years until 1901–the longest reign in British history.

- **Victoria's reign** is called the Victorian Age.

- **In the Victorian Age,** Britain became the world's largest industrial and trading power and the British Empire reached its peak.

- **British factories and towns** mushroomed and railways were built throughout the country.

- **In 1851,** the Great Exhibition opened in a huge building of glass and iron, later called the Crystal Palace, to show British skills to the world.

- **In 1861,** Victoria's husband, Prince Albert, died and she went into mourning and wore black the rest of her life.

▲ *Under Queen Victoria, Britain came to wield control over the largest empire the world had ever seen, and made astonishing artistic, scientific and manufacturing advances.*

▶ *Benjamin Disraeli, twice prime minister in Victorian England (1868 and 1874-1880), and one of Victoria's favourite statesmen. Under Disraeli, the British Empire gained even more status when Victoria became Empress of India.*

- **The rapid expansion** of Victorian cities created vast slum areas where living conditions were appalling.

- **Social reformers** and writers such as Charles Dickens highlighted the problems of the slums. Slowly, Parliament passed laws to improve conditions for working people and to provide education for all.

- **The two great** prime ministers of the Victorian Age were the flamboyant Benjamin Disraeli (1804–81) and the dour William Gladstone (1809–98).

- **Victorian middle-class life** cultivated cosy moral values, but there was also a seamy side, with widespread prostitution and crime.

35

World War I

- **World War I** (1914–18), the Great War, was the worst the world had seen (World War II would prove to be worse), killing 10 million troops.

- **The war was caused** by the rivalry between European powers in the early 1900s. The assassination of Franz Ferdinand in Sarajevo, Balkans, on 28 June 1914 made Austria start a war with Serbia. Russia came to Serbia's defence. Germany declared war on Russia and her ally France on 3 August.

- **The Germans** had a secret plan (the 'Schlieffen plan') for invading France. Instead of tackling the French head-on, as expected, they swept round to the north through neutral Belgium. This outrage drew Britain into the war.

- **As the Germans** moved into France, they came up against the British and French (the Allies). The opposing armies dug trenches – and stayed facing each other in much the same place for four years. The trenches, known as the Western front, stretched from the English Channel to Switzerland.

- **The war soon** developed an Eastern front, where the Central Powers (Austria and Germany) faced the Russians. The deaths of millions of Russians provoked the 1917 Revolution, which took Russia out of the war.

- **In the Alps** the Central Powers were opposed by Italy. At Gallipoli in Turkey, British and Anzac (Australia and New Zealand) troops fought the Turks.

- **The Allies** relied on supplies from N. America, so the Germans used submarines to attack ships. The sinking of the *Lusitania* in May 1915, with 128 Americans out of 1198 casualties, brought the USA into the war.

- **In 1918** there were 3.5 million Germans on the Western front and in March they broke through towards Paris.

- **In July** British tanks broke the German line at Amiens.

- **An Allied naval blockade** meant many people were starving in Germany. As more US troops arrived, the Germans were pushed back. At 11 o'clock on 11 November 1918, the Germans signed an armistice (peace).

◀ *Trenches were dug to protect troops from enemy gunfire, but became hell-holes, filled with water, rats and disease. Soldiers had to eat, sleep and stand guard ankle-deep in mud. Every now and then, they were ordered to 'go over the top' – climb out of their trenches and advance towards enemy lines. Out of the trench, they were exposed to enemy fire, and quickly mown down. Millions of soldiers on both sides died. On 1 July 1916, 60,000 British soldiers were killed in just a few hours in the Battle of the Somme. The four-month Somme offensive killed 600,000 Germans, 400,000 British and 200,000 French – and advanced the Allies 7 km. The horror of war was conveyed in letters and poems by soldiers such as Siegfried Sassoon and Wilfred Owen.*

World War II

- **World War II** (1939–45) was the most terrible war ever fought. It not only killed 17 million soldiers – compared to 10 million in World War I – but also twice as many civilians, through starvation, bombings and massacres.

- **It was the first** truly global war – fought on the plains of Europe, in the jungles of Southeast Asia, on the deserts of Africa, among the islands of the Pacific, on (and under) the Atlantic Ocean, and in many other places.

- **It began** when Hitler's Germany invaded Poland on 1 September 1939. Great Britain thought the USSR would defend Poland but Hitler and Stalin made a pact. As Germany invaded Poland from the west, the USSR invaded from the east.

- **After a lull,** or 'Phoney War', in May-June 1940, the Germans quickly overran Norway and Denmark, then Luxembourg, the Netherlands, Belgium and France.

- **The British army** was trapped by the Channel coast, but the Germans held back, and 338,000 British troops got away from Dunkirk, France, on an armada of little boats.

'Never in the field of human conflict have so many owed so much to so few' – Churchill on the British fighter pilots.

▶ *Winston Churchill (1874–1965) was the British prime minister whose courage and inspiring speeches helped the British withstand the German threat.*

▶ *The bombing of Pearl Harbour by the Japanese forced the US to enter the war. Almost 4000 people were killed or injured by the attack, with the main targets being US war ships.*

- **By August 1940,** Italy joined the war on the German side, and Germany launched air raids on England to prepare for an invasion. This was the Battle of Britain (above).

- **Fearing the USSR** would turn against him, Hitler launched a sudden invasion of the USSR on 22 June 1941. The USA joined the war when Japan bombed its fleet without warning in Pearl Harbor, Hawaii, on 7 Dec 1941.

- **Germany, Italy, Japan** and six other nations joined forces as the 'Axis'. Britain, the USA, USSR, China and 50 other nations were together called the Allies. In 1942, the Allies halted the Axis in Africa, invading Italy in 1943 and France in 1944. In 1945, the Allies drove into Germany from east and west. Germany surrendered on 7 May 1945. The terrible Pacific conflict ended when the USA dropped atom bombs on the Japanese cities Hiroshima and Nagasaki. Japan surrendered on 2 Sept 1945.

- **As the Allies** moved into Germany, they found the horror of Nazi death camps like Auschwitz and Buchenwald, where millions of Jews and others had been slaughtered by starvation and in gas chambers.

> **. . . FASCINATING FACT . . .**
> The key to the early German successes was the Blitzkrieg ('lightning war')
> – a stunningly rapid attack with tanks and aeroplanes.

Index